In Times of Terror, Wage Beauty

Collaboration by **Wage Beauty** and **Think Disrupt**
Designed by: Melissa Athina
Published by **Wage Beauty** x **Think Disrupt**
©Copyright 2014. All rights reserved.

Think Disrupt
Co-founder / CEO Hodan Ibrahim
Co-Founder / Creative Director Melissa Athina
A new media publishing company serving the create
maladjustment of the nonconforming minority.
thinkdisrupt.ca

Wage Beauty
Founder / CEO Mark Gonzales
We are a creative leadership agency with a simple purpose:
to design & deliver inspiration wherever invited and
whenever neccesary.
wagebeauty.com

dedication

What you are holding in your hand are ideas in
story form that I've learned on this journey called my life.

What you are also holding is people, the visually curated
memory of dreams of all I've crossed paths with who've
touched my heart and inspired my spine.

Grateful to all who contributed to the collage of
visions I am determined to advance.

Grateful to all those who will carry forward the ideas I've
laid out in this book and my life.

As I look at the world today, I am aware of how miniscule
one person may seem to the systemic actions in front of
our eyes yet, oddly, I ask you to laugh at such shrinking of
our potential. For the Divine does not make mistakes and
nearly every sacred tradition says we who exist were imagined
since the beginning of time.

What does that mean? Simple.

We were made for this moment.

table of contents

Even when your breath seems weak & quivering, give thanks. Wounded though an exhale may be, it is scientific proof we are still amongst the land of the living.

That alone is reason for hope.

chapter 1

GROW WINGS

USE THEM

lend them to others

Gravity is an illusion to we who are born of starlight and thermodynamics. For what is starlight but energy? What are humans but energy? What is the 2nd law of thermodynamics but a reminder that energy cannot be created or destroyed?

What are we then loved ones, but infinite.

Is there chaos in the finite? Yes, for what else would you call a structural gravity that attempts to hold us down and prevent starlight from dancing in the cosmos.

This is why whenever possible, grow wings, even if you are the only one who can see them.
For wings are a metaphysical metaphor for refusing to be held down in a world where there are so many stars to explore.

11

In this moment, an echo is occurring across the globe. It is the human spirit craving to be reminded one does not need permission to grow.

In this moment an echo is occurring across our hearts. It is the realization that love has its own logic.

Live. Love. Grow. Even if one cannot make life more beautiful, at least make it more bearable. This should be considered the base for being human.

May the passion continue. May the circle expand.

chapter 2

we weren't made in America

WE MADE

AMERICA

The question of how human beings learn to be who they think they are has always fascinated me. So much of our understanding of identity mirrors product development concepts, where we stamp humans by place of origin and the date of manufacturing.

Origin: the place one begins. This could be such a fascinating ecosystem of conversations.
Sadly, it is now flattened to a nation state and color coded passports.

What a boring way of engaging human experience.

The effect of this mentality is most evident in those of us who have either had our lands of origin invaded, or were forced out of them. These series of displacements thrust us into a world where we are continually expected to explain ourselves, our identity, and our origin.

Those who've never lived inside a body that is constantly under interrogation do not know how emotionally and mentally draining it is.

Yet the most tragic part of chronic interrogation is this: as long as we spend the vast amount of our days answering the questions being asked by others we have no time or energy left to ask our own.

Am I an American? What a boring question. Ask if I'm a lover, a dreamer, a present father, a decent son.

Am I British? Frances? Australian? Was I manufactured here? Am I a bio-toy to have my country of origin embedded on my belly?

Truth is, I am many things, and one of them is a
word that has not yet been invented. One that
articulates the generational journeys that lead up to
this moment called now. I don't know what to call us,
we whose identities have been denied citizenship,
we who were forced arrivals, who became new
neighbors, who became blended with those who
were here before a country was.

We are an ancient people, a mosaic of genes and
dreams and all other human elements of beautiful
beings who were stolen and who were occupied.

Where are I from? To be honest, due to erasure of
stories and language, I can only travel back so far.
What can tell you is this: even if we weren't made in
America, we made America.

chapter 3

APOLOGIZE TO YOUR
ancestors

THEN APOLOGIZE TO YOUR
dreams

WHEN DONE, LOOK IN THE
mirror:

APOLOGIZE TO
yourself.

If you are one who feels defeated, encourage you
to hold a mirror to what we victoriously survived
over the last five centuries. As people who live in
difficult times, we can never have enough reminders
of human beings who embodied resilience and
cultivated goodness.

Feelings of frustration are natural. Yet when isolated,
then compounded across generational traumas, they
can metastasize into an inferiority complex for an
entire people.

Reflect on the genetic journey of millennium that
led into you. Listen to your lungs. How powerful is
your breath for even being able to hold air with the
weight of Empires that have attempted to impede that
natural process of inhale, exhale, breathe.

Listen to your heart. Give thanks to those who came
before, then leave behind a little more than what you
were given. Do not limit intelligence to solely the
mind. Be a genius of heart. Your genetics already are.
Playing small only benefits your enemies.

Say it with me:
Now is not the time to be timid.
Now is not the time to be timid.
Now is not the time to be timid.

chapter 4

A BETTER WORLD

begins with a

BETTER STORY

An integral part of nurturing a culture of storytelling into one's lungs, family or society is simply this: tell your story.

For story is a uniquely creative curation of ideas innate to the human species. It is the primary way we shape collective memory and blueprint futures via language that is visual, written, spoken, danced, or embodied.

Stories do more than articulate reality. They create it, shape the geography of imagination our ideas live upon, and place emotions inside another person's heart. They spark imagination in ways that call us to transform ourselves or our world. This is why a better world begins with a better story.

Sadly, too many of us were conditioned within decades of a lifetime, or even over centuries, to bury our words in our throat. Now our lungs have become cemeteries of memory and story. As such, we have normalized someone else's version of the past, and have already surrendered our future.

Speak now. Speak often. In a world of forced silence, it is a microstrategy step towards the reclaiming of voice. Yet always remember: it is not enough to teach soft voices how to speak. We must teach loud voices how to listen.

I, for one, do not want to live in a world where my father has to shout in order to be heard.

chapter 5

We are not the children
nor the descendants
of a weak people.

An essential component of healing the hearts of those
forced from their homelands: center their beauty. It
is simple approach to disrupting that loop tape of self
deprecation that is playing on repeat in so many of
our brains.

For there are few pains distinct as the one that
emerges from a feeling of abnormality, that seemingly
inescapable idea that one is all alone in their wound
and this world. Scaled up, it becomes a social belief
present across hearts that one's pain has no parallels,
perpetuating feelings of shame and isolation.

My, how trauma convinces us we are abandoned.
It is an unimaginative composer corrupting that loop
tape that sits in your frontal lobe, impeding our
ability to see beyond our own experience, much
less across generations.

Look up. Look around. Listen. See and hear the echoes of your wounds and dreams all around you. Know that you are never alone as you think. We may even be in the majority. Each point of connection with another transforms them from stranger into ally In the healing process.

If you read this and still feel abandoned, walk with head high knowing there are generations of ancestors inside of you. We will survive this era as we did the eras before: using the skills we have, inventing the ones we need.

On those days when the spine or soul becomes tired, imagine all of humanity whispering a twelve word prayer inside your ear: "we are not the children nor the descendants of a weak people".

chapter 6

the time for silence is over.

if you love something,

SPEAK LOUD & SPEAK OFTEN

Your life is a story arch. We are prologue, living literature placed after all that ever was. We are prelude, opening the chapter of infinity to all that will ever be. What occurs between these two spaces in this moment called now will be penned by what is within. May we be bold, bliss, & loving.

Bigots have become increasingly loud these days, their decibels an attempt to mask how unimaginative their ideas are. Our continual silence is a white flag surrendering of story & imagination to them.

Pick up your tongue off the floor. Take it off the shelf. From under the bed. Aim it intentionally at silence and ignorance. Speak.

If you are one who nurtures other's stories, please remember language is more than idea in sound, it is a terrain. As such, to speak for someone is to be more than rude, it is to invade.

For lovers of life & language who desire to be an ally of the human heart through story should know it is not only what you say, but knowing when to lower voice and be silent.

Let go of the doubt in the power of your story, even if it seems miniscule. Let go of the doubt in the power of your voice, even if you believe it is a whisper.

For even if your contribution to a better world seems like a small step, never doubt the power of a micro-strategy done with a macro-intent.

chapter 7

IF NO ONE HAS TOLD YOU,

YOUR DESIRE TO HEAL IS

so damn beautiful

EVEN WHEN THE WAY YOU'VE

TRIED TO HEAL YOUR WOUNDS IS

FLAWED

What is your first memory of love? What was your first memory of a love that deeply wounded you? What is your dream for a love that makes your back arch and your soul smile?

If the first two questions are traumatizing ones, turn towards the third. Engage, embody, and advance.

Yes, memory is an essential terrain to reclaim & heal. Yet it is a part of infinity, not the entirety. We are always more than what was done to us. This is why if one feels weak when looking back at the past, look towards the future. Imagine it as the space where there will be a positive reconciliation between your soul and your self. Begin to map your journey there.

It would not be unfathomable to conceive that in the midst of all the abuses a previous lover was committing upon the flesh of your tapestry, they failed to mention: your breath is more than the echo of infinity, it is the medium through which it will be amplified.

This is why for you who battle with self-doubt and hyper criticism, I remind you we are a generation experimenting with healing in public. Be fierce. Be forgiving. Hardcore is a facade and a trend.

Long live the children of fierce vulnerability.

chapter 8

Stories are the engine of identity. Stories are the engine of identity.

Despite the continual academic references to it predominately as a performative act, stories are more than pretty phonemes dancing on tongues that have this amazing ability to entertain.

They are the vessels for ancestors, memory, futures, and laughter. They are the medium through which the divine is engaged. They are the primary way through which human beings learn how to be a specific type of human.

To state it more succinctly, stories are ceremony.

For language is how humans architect time and shape imagination. Each word is either bridge or border. This is why new language is essential. Who amongst us doesn't desire a new playground to explore the future in, one not so weighed down with bigoted beliefs.

41

What is 'new language' but a new generational lexicon through which we explore identity & ideas of difference. This is what our generation will be known for, our innovations in a playground of sound. Let them roll off your tongue, down your lungs, into your face & dreams till you redefine what it means to be.

This playground will be open to all, and benefit more than any specific sector. It will transform our understanding of human behavior on every level.

For stories are the engine of identity. Language is the mechanics that construct our ideas of self and other. Our love is the space fuel. Our imagination is the map that guides across this road trip of life. We are the drivers and star light navigators. Now is the time to drive courageously.

chapter 9

WE **CANNOT** HEAL WHAT
WE **WILL** NOT FACE

Before the tears have dried on your cheek, the next bruise on your arms, the next atrocity is on the television screen, promise me you will not turn away from what we must face.

Is it difficult? Absolutely. Especially when we see the same betrayals occurring over and over again. Yet one of the greatest acts of courage is not an external one, but internal. It is learning to trust (again). We will begin with ourselves.

In this moment, we renew our commitment to finding a cure for self-harm by directly addressing the origins of self-hate.

Touch your skin. Is it shaking? Do not judge yourself for feeling fearful. For the fear one feels facing the unknown is quiet natural. What is fear but emotion, and what is emotion but a reminder we are human.

Draw a through line between your life and wounds and others. Not only across a community, but across time. Look at how many of us there are. When a pain exceeds a person and enters the realm of millions, then our wounds are not a problem but a symptom.

Without the knowledge there are so many echoes of our lived experience, we will continue to sit in silence believing our wounds are abnormal versus systemic. As such, somehow they will always be beyond 'repair'.

If there are those who actively deny a space for us to speak about our pain, let them know that a community which habitually avoids speaking on doubts, dreams or other substantive dialogues is one that still has its trainer wheels on.

Speak your truth & your life. It is a micro-step to ending a culture of shame that keeps depression, chemical imbalance, and suicide silent.

We are not ugly because we are wounded. What is ugly are those who inflict scars on innocence. Beautiful is we who endured what was inflicted and are reclaiming our self, our sanity, and our future. This is what it means to wage beauty, to embrace ourselves in personal and structural ways that transform a world of wounds into one that is nurturing.

For we have vastly limited the definition of healing, loved ones. It is not merely the absence of pain, it is the presence of pleasure.

chapter 10

Educate
the
Human Heart
Elevate
the
Human Mind
Grow the
Human Soul

What better way is there to shift a paradigm than by speaking in ways that encourage dreams, laughter and imagination. For those acts of creativity are not luxury, short sighted or simplistic, they are essential.

A society that does not value imagination is one that has ensured its future will be a clone of its present traumas. This is why the global shift in the pitch of our generational frequency is so wondrous. If you have not heard, we are embracing a discourse of dreams and dignity versus one solely of struggle.

Yes, whenever possible a human being should read poetry. Yes, whenever possible, one should write poetry. Yet above all we must commit to living poetically, as frequent as humanly possible. This is how we introduce invention into existence.

The first sign of any paradigm shift is when a language or framework is being echoed by people in separate parts of a planet who've never met.

The second comes when intentional introductions are made, relationships blossom, and a new belief system begins to emerge from the cross pollination of best practices and fabulous failures.

Be bold with your dreams in this moment, even as you are patient with one another. For how do we heal a society so addicted to disposable culture, we discard relationships due to convenience? Continual intentional friendships that abandon the frameworks of toxic interactions.

Educate the human heart. Elevate the human mind. Grow the human soul. This will be our generation's idea of a multi-tasking model of learning.

chapter 11

**A CULTURE THAT IS
NOT IN CONTROL OF
THEIR OWN NARRATIVE
WILL FOREVER
LIVE AT THE MERCY**
of another's pen.

In the most innovative frameworks, those who use narrative in social transformation see storytelling as a medium to map community experiences through a process that is culturally centered, attractive, and accessible.

Within that moment, the philosophy of story no longer becomes confined to a page. The map becomes a language based assessment of how people perceive their own wounds, needs, and dreams. Every human than becomes a storyteller and a story creator.

In this collective environment, an isolated story transforms into a personalized submission into an anthology of shared experiences and unique memories. With each new telling, we cocoon to butterfly that sees each breath we have left in this life as an exercise in evolving our own narrative.

This is why it is essential we see narrative as a concept that means more than a collection of stories. It is the thread that curates previously isolated stories into an anthology to advance a system of values. Such a thread guides our understanding of ourselves, as well as each other.

Sadly, in this specific moment in time, narratives have become pop culture quilts woven by those who have little respect for the linguistic fabric that transforms random strangers into a community of shared responsibility. This must be reversed.

The finite could never destroy the infinite, their only hope of victory was to steal the children of angels and teach them self-destruction. This began with the theft of our language, and continues with the theft of our pens.

Now, like every moment before it, is the time to tell our stories. Simultaneously, we must create spaces to cultivate the skill sets that invite our loved ones to do the same. We must do so in ways that explores words, versus blindly parrots, patrols or invades them.

Failure to do so will continue a social discourse that values monologues over conversations, and forced silenced over participatory storytelling.

As it is with language, so it is with life.

chapter 12

YOU ARE MORE THAN
THE SUM OF WHAT
CAME BEFORE. $\sqrt{}$ *You are the square root of what will come after.*

To all the new creative lovers of life, the idea design minded, the wounded but healing, you are more than welcome here. You are invited.

Know that if even the very physical nature of this world is impermanent, there is no way a wound could be infinite. Every scar will one day be the place where a future garden will grow.

Let go of the paralysis of analysis that has us so consumed with fear of death and loss that we forget to live. Unacceptable.

We lost many along the way, but the reality is if you are reading this, then the world could not kill us all.

Time is infinite, as are we. For one of the most powerful ideas a human being could ever engage is how we are far from dust in the wind powerless. We are the pivot point between all that ever was (ancestors) and all that ever will be (generations to come). Who are we then but ancestors in training.

For when you look up at the stars then look down at the land, you realize even if a day comes where we are the last one on this earth, being absolutely abandoned is impossible.

Our family is the universe.

chapter 13

CHANGE
the STORY
CHANGE THE GAME

Before one can shift social discourse, they must engage what a story is, why collections of them matter to people & how to author one that speaks to the heart in ways that fear cannot silence.

Every word is a portal into understanding, shape your vocabulary in a way that maximizes possibility. Be aware of how the language you use can be counterproductive to the world your vision is attempting to grow.

Reaction is so 20th century. Upgrade your stories, upgrade your language. For my prayer for us is this: there will come a day where we learn that a language of growth fits our souls far better than a language of resistance.

Look back across time. We were not designed to resist, but to create and affirm. A newborn does not enter this life with a desire to heal, but to thrive and activate their fullest potential.

Resistance has too often become a reactionary rebranding of the acts we have always done to defend and grow our people.

Encourage you all to not be passive members in the story of family, or the narrative of society. Listen. Author. Amplify.

A people who are continually placed on the defensive will be forced to reallocate time best spent imagining into responding.

Change the story. Change the game. Prioritize dreaming.

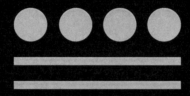

chapter 14

Look Up

SEE THAT SHINING & BRILLIANCE DEFYING OF GRAVITY?

THOSE ARE NOT ONLY STARS. THEY ARE OUR RELATIVES

The most valuable lesson I learned from sitting with elders across the globe is the importance of taking time while they are still present. For while it may seem hard to hear or heal a wounded story, a buried story is far more difficult to resurrect.

When listening know there is more than phonemes being shared. Stories are time machines, they transport us to spaces we have been stripped of where we can be amongst loved ones.

It is a way of visiting the cemeteries so many of us have been banned from.

Visit your elders, and know they are more than those who are older who share the same blood. There are elders of love and of genre. There are elders younger than you. There are elders you can only visit in dreams.

Visit them all. Learn their stories. We are never as alone as we think.

chapter 15

THE ROLE OF CREATIVE LANGUAGE IN SOCIAL CHANGE IS THIS:
CREATE A NARRATIVE FOR A NEW WORLD SO BRILLIANT
IT RENDERS THE CURRENT ONE OBSOLETE.

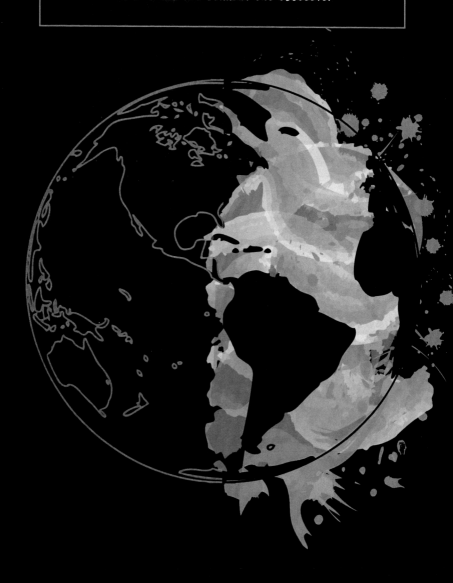

Language as a tool of creation has a unique ability to carry with it more than a visual economy of places we've been. It articulates bridges to every place we have yet to go & to every person we have yet to meet.

This is why it is knife to heart difficult to hear so many conversations engage ideas that do not excite the human soul. They render potentially black hole powerful words as monochromatic bland.

Even the way we define words do not serve dignity to the beauty they are attempting to hold. When did the definition of belonging become imprisoned to ideas of citizenship? When did our definition of wealth become limited to the realm of finance versus what a person or a people value?

Yet what is most stagnant is our ability to create. It is as if we have forgotten that one does not shift a narrative by responding to it. One shifts by authoring a new narrative so brilliant it makes the existing one look painfully unimaginative and obviously bigoted.

Towards the new.

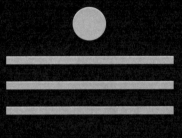

chapter 16

GROW

THAT IS WHAT THIS MOMENT IS FOR.
CONCRETE & BARBED WIRE BE DAMNED.

The curves in your palm are more than wrinkles in skin, they are the genetic terrain through which we can trace back all those who ever lived in our hands.

How limited our belief in our own brilliance has become. Traumatized by moments and millenniums, we have become shortsighted, afraid of our own shadows and the sound of a whisper. Remind yourself how vast are all those who comprised your family. How much more so then are those who comprise your culture?

Head up, face forward. One of the greatest acts of creativity an individual can learn is the art of avoiding a momentary setback becoming a cycle of self-defeat.

Possibility is a universe written in eleven letters. May your life be a love affair with its definition, embodied and advanced with each breath.

Context is what enables us to remember we have survived far worse than this present moment, & we will grow something far better.

May we never imprison ourselves to the confining parameters of what our current society tells us is possible. For this is a fate worse than death.

There are nine words that comprise three separate three word mantras that are the secret to our genetic resilience. Learn them. Live them. Say them.

We will heal. We will grow. We will win.

chapter 17

IS A WORD THAT IS IN DESPERATE NEED OF
BEING DISMANTLED AND TRANSFORMED.

There are few words that are so often articulated yet rarely defined as the term "power." In the instances its done so, it implies participation in electoral politics or an abundance in salary. Rarely does it mean the ability to affect life expectancy or quality of life.

For what is power as a frequency but the ability to organize bodies into conditions of premature death or extended spaces of life. What is power as a form but the way that frequency operates across personal, structural and collective spheres.

What then, shall we say is the power of language? Speaking social linguistically, power is the ability to create a monopoly on definitions and normalize them in the consciousness of an entire population. It is the ability to create the default image that appears in our brain when we hear words like 'love', 'success', or even 'human'.

Such a looking glass world this is, societies arrogantly defining identities they do not embrace. Now is the time to reclaim our right to define the words we use, especially the ones we embody.

In doing so, perhaps this word called "man" will realize being a better lover and father doesn't require us abandoning our manhood. On the contrary, it consists of us evolving the definition of it.

This word called "economy" will understand emotional intelligence is the underpinnings of the entire future of entrepreneurship.

Language will no longer be confused by bigots or borders as the term "indigenous" will again refer to genetic origins in a region, not one's generational birth place.

The value in the phonemes that form the word "woman" will not be confined to quantifiable labor or the ability to be in labor, but a human being capable of dreaming.

For the trap too many generations fell in before us was attempting to seize power, versus transform the ways it was defined and distributed. May we be far more imaginative and successful than our predecessors.

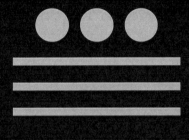

chapter 18

ISN'T LIMITED TO THE MIND OR BODY
OF A SINGULAR PERSON. IT HAS
THE ABILITY TO HAVE A CUMULATIVE
IMPACT ON AN ENTIRE PEOPLE

In the last century alone, trauma foundations have undergone four drastic shifts, from the physical to the psychological to the post-traumatic. The fourth is what we are witnessing now.

For within western psychology frameworks, trauma is primarily examined often through the lens of the individual. Rarely is it seen as collective wound that dramatically reshapes the interactions and wellbeing of an entire people.

It is as if we have forgotten human beings are, at our core essence, social creatures. How then could we ever limit our ideas of pain, much less the ways to resolve them, to a singular individual.

Neuroscience and sacred traditions both tell us that genetics carry physiological and emotional coding that we pass on to our children. When their children move from womb to world, and have children of their own, that genetic memory will not be buried, but encoded. Reflect on that for a moment.

When an entire society is desecrated, demonized, invaded, or imprisoned, it reshapes the cultural gene pool of that entire generation. What is trauma then, but a collective and a cumulative phenomenon.

Our progress in healing and preventing trauma will grow exponentially when we begin to see scars as collective wounds versus an individual's "issues". For no matter your pain, there is at least one person walking with a parallel wound.

Perhaps now you understand why on stage so many of us say: these are not poems but the story based strategy of healing the wounds of an invaded people. The truth is our generation is not sad, nor are we apathetic. We are suffering from intergenerational shell shock.

May these words help you move beyond numbness. I too am learning to let go of the hate for one's self that emerges from continually being subjected to a social narrative of invisibility or demonization.

We as a generation are learning certain things we were never meant to own. Shame, emerging from a wrong that was done to us, is one of them.

We will build like we love: intensely, imaginatively, and intentionally. All else will follow.

There are those who want the world to remain on its current path. This is not only unacceptable, it is painfully unimaginative. For the beauty of our generation is we are uniquely situated to achieve what so many in this world currently consider impossible. How exquisitely beautiful it will be to watch the current narrative go down in flames, then witness poetics & phoenix rise from the ashes.

Embers, ancestors, and angels await us loved ones. Forward.

biography

Mark Gonzales is the CEO of the *Institute of Narrative Growth* and the Chief Storyteller for multiple start ups. Aggregating human centered design with transformative narratives, he has launched pop up universities across the globe for every day people to unlock human potential.

His expertise is informed from fifteen years of professional experiences that span five continents, with clients as diverse as Ivy League Universities, refugee camps, creative agencies, corporate executives, and first time fathers like himself.